DEERHART

YVONNE REDDICK

KFS

NEWTON-LE-WILLOWS

Published in the United Kingdom in 2016
by The Knives Forks And Spoons Press,
122 Birley Street,
Newton-le-Willows,
Merseyside,
WA12 9UN.

ISBN 978-1-909443-65-5

Copyright © Yvonne Reddick, 2016.

The right of Yvonne Reddick to be identified as the author of this work has been asserted by her in accordance with the Copyrights, Designs and Patents act of 1988. All rights reserved. No part of this publication may be reproduced, stored in a retrieval system, transmitted in any form or by any means, electronic, photocopying, recording or otherwise, without prior permission of the publisher.

Acknowledgments:

Devil's Thunderbolt – *English* (Oxford Journals) 63. 242 (Autumn 2014): 224.

Poem For 'Eva' – special issue of *The Clearing*, August 2014, dedicated to Yvonne Reddick's poetry.

Trilobite – Yvonne Reddick, *LandForms* (Orkney: Seapressed, 2012).

Ermine Street – commended in the York Literature Festival Poetry Competition 2015 and published at http://www.yorkmix.com/things-to-do/poetry/the-yorkmix-york-literature-festival-poetry-competition-read-the-winners/.

Chillán Fruit Basket for Pablo – *Tears in the Fence* 61 (Winter/Spring 2015): 68.

Deerhart – *Interdisciplinary Studies in Literature and the Environment* 22.2 (Winter 2015): 2-3.

How It Feels - *Interdisciplinary Studies in Literature and the Environment* 22.2 (Winter 2015): 5.

My Grandmother Was A Pink-Footed Goose won third prize in the *Sentinel Literary Quarterly* Competition, January 2015, and was published in *Sentinel Literary Quarterly* in February 2015 here: http://sentinelquarterly.com/2015/02/yvonne-reddick/

Cover Image: 'Hunting the Bride' by Diana Zwibach

Table of Contents

Devil's Thunderbolt	5
Poem For 'Eva'	6
Trilobite	7
I Redecorate My House To Resemble *La Cueva de Tito Bustillo*	8
Ermine Street	9
The Black Drop	10
Chillán Fruit Basket for Pablo	11
Sylvia's Plait	12
Lined Notebook, Slight Foxing	13
The Migration of Tundra Swans	14
Deerhart	15
How It Feels	16
Totem	17
L'Art de vénerie	18
Trash	19
Sorrows of the Deer	20
My Grandmother Was A Pink-Footed Goose	22

Devil's Thunderbolt

At a cliff's foot
I hunt ammonites
in fissile layers
of flaky silt-beds.

But a belemnite
tight as a rifle bullet,
finds me.

I turn it between fingers.
Thick and unwieldy
as the graphite-tipped stub
that rounded my first
laborious letters.

It's an inch-long pen,
but lightning-acute.
No wonder Whitby dialect
calls it a 'devil's thunderbolt' –

it writes miniscules,
eyes mouth muscles,
pennate tentacles,

writhes on the page,
unspools an inky sea,

hides in its own essence,
leaving this shale core.

Each time I think
I've grasped it,
it swims away

into itself.

Yvonne Reddick

Poem For 'Eva'

I've got a delicate paintbrush, a dentist's water-pick, and several kilos of high explosive.

Now that I've found you, it's time to awaken you
by blasting you out of your deep-sunk bed.

You are
         crumbling
                 as I touch the rust-scented marl
holding your white fragments
              in a curl of the river Aude.
This bone bed was once a riverbed, meander laving your relics, gravels inurning you.

I dig a turtle's scute,
       your humerus,
            your scattered vertebrae
– finally your face –
                  out of the Upper Cretaceous.

I wrap your limbs in plaster bandages. The plaster dries, ossifies.
Your arm-bone, long and thick as my leg, white encased in white.

Painfully, carefully, I stick your bones' fibres together,
fix limbs in sockets, root each tooth, lock the links of your spine.

We stand, poised, on the edge of aeons. You watch me patiently from your afterlife.

Trilobite

Curled like a human embryo –
compound eyes blank with mineral dreams.
Its frail armour still braced

to endure the undersea sandstorm.
Scales and ringmail of fragile chitin
could not deflect the grinding pressures
of silt-layers crushed into shale.

You can feel
the sand's weight entombing it alive
as it rests in your warm,
nerved hand.

Yvonne Reddick

I Redecorate My House To Resemble
La Cueva de Tito Bustillo

I need the darkness to breathe with beasts.
    First, I let the Rivers Moru, Noceu, San Miguel and crazy Llocu in through the roof. Their muttering soothes my sleep. I sledgehammer the bathroom ceiling, let faithful rains sculpt flowstone waterfalls and gours with step-lipped mouths in the en suite. With my shower dripping, water dissolves the bricks and rebuilds them as stalactites. All light fittings must be ripped out, and the broadband cancelled.
    Lastly, I outline a reindeer's armature of antlers in black manganese; sketch a horned aurochs head, carbon-dark; daub violet clay for the bristling mane of a tarpan. I bathe the wall of my makeshift cavern in blood-rust ochre.
    They are summoned. I listen at the splintered window for their extinct hooves to come quaking the tarmac of Hamilton Drive.

Ermine Street

Tonight, while men drink Guzzler
in the Old Black Swan
and women with rosé lips
check their phones,

the Ninth marches north
from Lindum to Eboracum
with a flare of bronze trumpets.
Their steel-hooped corselets
glint in the moonlight.

At their head rides Martius Vitalis, *centurio*,
on a tall battle-horse with shaggy fetlocks.
Duccius Rufinus hoists the standard.

As they file along Blossom Street
and cross the Ouse,
a lad in Lendal Cellars chokes on his beer.
At the Porta Praetoria
they stride in formation
beneath the Yorkshire Insurance Building.

Listen. Muffled war-songs
to the tramp of hobnailed sandals
from eighteen feet below the city.

Tired auxiliaries follow Stonegate,
trudge through the cellar
of the Treasurer's House –
a guy fixing the plumbing falls off his ladder.
They slog through the opposite wall
and troop northeast along the Via Decumana.

At the barracks, they strip
tunics and armour,
soothe their limbs in the *caldarium*'s steam.
A whiff of warm vapour in the Roman Bath Pub –
the pint Jade's pulling overflows
as she and Felicius Simplex clock each other.
He's stark naked. Their jaws fall.

Tomorrow night,
the legion leaves towered fastness
for the cold hills of the Picti
beyond the Wall.

Yvonne Reddick

The Black Drop

I brush aside a single yellow poppy,
open the leadlight window.
To my right you sit
in your portrait, opposite your friend's
ivory scales and your vial
labelled *Lancashire Genuine Black Drop*.

Your skin's *thoughtful bloom*
grown florid, corpulent.
You look to one side,
lips *gross, voluptuous,*
parted as if speaking to thin air.
A puckered brow under *floating hair*.
You were too ill to finish sitting –
friends thought your mouth and nose
fabrications.

If I'd been here when you were here
I'd grow bruise-petalled poppies outside the cottage,
make codeine for your cough,
morphine for your rheumatism –
swap your *free-agency-annihilating*
opium for methadone.
I'd pity you.

On the mantelpiece downstairs
someone has left an offering
of eight brittle poppy seed-husks.

Chillán Fruit Basket for Pablo

Full woman, carnal apple, warm moon,
thick smell of seaweed –
and you, Neruda, what primal fruit are *you* hiding?

Come on, women are *Mississippis of apples*,
not *ancient nights*. Your affairs scorched,
 a flash in the dark. Mine strike taproots,
unfurl the years till their branches fill continents.

My man sleeps, curled alone in his lair of dusk.
I kiss a faltering path through soft animal smells
to the citrus tang of his mouth.
He's awkward as a *scruffy chestnut*

so I steal your inkwell, your trick of writing in green,
and he rouses to the feel of feeling skin.
Flesh smelts to flesh, skin welds to tongue –
till the sun ignites its dawn peach.

When the singed core cools
I'll let it sprout and root an orchard.
We'll bicker as our gnarled hands prune and pick
but we'll wreathe close as a pleached thicket.

Keep your *cellular grapes, submarine figs,*
rotten *carnal apples*. Leave me some pips.

Yvonne Reddick

Sylvia's Plait

You pick through boxes of her oval writing
and stumble on the casket that holds her hair.
Warily, you lift the lid.

It was styled to a wavy Veronica Lake bang
when she posed with an upside-down rose –
you'd never know it bandaged the trenched scar
of thirty-six hours in a coma underworld.

It swung loose in that platinum summer of 1954
when her limbs were long and brazen
in a white bathing suit and all American smile.
After prom-dates with Yale sophomores
and days hunched over Dostoevsky
it wound by her nape, a studious light brown.

At Cambridge, leggy shots for *Varsity*
show a luminary smile in lipstick
and pinned-up Betty Grable curls.
Still, her hair lures your gaze
from the Lilly's august portraits,
your half-written article on her likenesses.

The German Hausfrau style
of a tressed circlet once she'd married –
in Devon, braids were the look for a country wife,
carefully twined in the photo with the babies
on a turf mound that erupts daffodils.

She grins, but her eyes stare gravely
from her son's face; her bun an unravelling nimbus
in 1962, when something came undone.
That winter, her hair hung lank, untressed.

How unlike the soft braid in your palm,
silky as if from a living head.
You run a fingertip along it. A jolt of static.
One strand comes unbound,
settles on the page of your notebook.

Lined Notebook, Slight Foxing
For Ted Hughes

I can hear you
through the page in front of me:
If you're going to do summat, do it good.

I watch your schoolboy copperplate
grow upright–
the strong curl of the *d* fishhooks back.

You cast the bait for words
while raindrops slur the ink
and you sketch the kypes and eyes of salmon.
You write yourself into the river.

Trails of ink are brush-marks in snow,
blots the impressions of paw-pads.
You wear the tod's fabled mask.

Now you've gone to ground
among these speckled leaves
where the dogs can't dig.

I stumble into your grimoire –
its briary symbols snag me.

You stand at my shoulder,
your laughter earth-deep and quiet.
Light fingermarks fox the page.

Yvonne Reddick

The Migration of Tundra Swans

Sir Peter inspects the sky
to the north-east, each October
for their return to Slimbridge.

At quarter past five on a December evening, he writes:

>*This is a proper relationship
>between man and bird.*

Aged eleven, Dafila knows a thousand by name.
Falcon holds the binoculars
as Sir Peter sketches the yolky tattoo of Rose Lee's bill.

He jots their portraits: full faces and profiles.

>*A large, very beautiful pen,*

Victoria's beak is high-bridged
with a regal black streak.

Jane Eyre is pinioned
and Lancelot's an unmistakable pennyface.
Pirate's a pinkneb, Spoony is round-headed –

>*friends who know us well by sight as individual humans
>whom they can trust.*

Caper sojourns in the Netherlands and Germany,
soars over the Elbe from East to West,
above the Iron Curtain.

>*These 'tundra swans', as they are called by the Soviets
>migrate from breeding grounds in the Arctic USSR.*

The Major, an imposing yellowneb,
devotes the summer of the Leningrad Affair
to raising his brood on the shore at Primorsk.

When Coddle is spotted in Novaya Zemlya
no-one mentions Robert Falcon Scott,
who skimmed the sea to the Beardmore Glacier
and Last Depôt, in the globe's other winter.

Deerhart

Dàmhair, 'rutting month'
at Loch an Daimh, the stag's loch.
Rust-flanked stags taste rivals
in the wind with stripped-back lips.
They catch my muffled footfalls
and stalk into the next glen.

I read limbs in prints
and spoor on burn-margins, peat-hags –
picture their eyes' startled intelligence.
They foil me, lose me
in the wood's antlered shadows.

I track their traces through myths
beast-musk rank with age.
Their hooves slot smoothly
into stories: a cross flares
between a white stag's horns.

These red deer are ghosts of Irish elk.
Weeds fur elk bones
under Hog Hole's peaty vault –
but a new fawn couches unseen in a covert.

Yvonne Reddick

How It Feels

Once from a leathery egg,
then each month from skin's flaked scales.

First I'll slough old age,
shuffle off its loose skeins.
Fold them away
with pastels and florals.

Unspool middle age, its sidewinding
stretch marks, thicker waist.
That skin peels into children
who drink youth through a curled cord.

Strip my twenties –
their silks and Lycra.
The empty sequins
of my sun-freckled scales will bask
on rocks with dry snakeskins.

I'll rush to peel away adolescence,
its constrictor grip, its whisperings.
Wriggle out of stretched, blemished skin.

I'll emerge
a child, watching damselfly nymphs
shed water, dry wings.

So this is how it feels to keep being born.

Totem

A black-lipped grin, then it ambled to the kitchen,
swiped a box of eggs and gulped them off the floor,
crunching the shells. It gnawed the frozen filet mignon
from my housemate's freezer drawer.

It gnarred, "Write about me.
When I bite I don't let go. So don't screw up",
yawned, then waited, eye-pupils slitted narrow.

I scrawled a poem, fast, about how
our relationship was ~~a nuisance~~ symbiotic, precious.
How its visits inspired ~~gave~~ me ~~night terrors for weeks~~.
How my boyfriend found it ~~disturbing~~ endearing
when it dozed on our bed, purred like a chainsaw.
I read the poem aloud and it stretched languorously,
turned to leave, and brushed its flank against my right arm.
Its markings burrowed into me, brindled my skin. They burned –
I scratched the branded parts till I bared blood.

Next morning, I woke with a roaring headache
and dog breath. A tameless stink had curled itself up in my sheets.
Something gritty had worked between my front teeth,
and a red gout that wasn't lipstick clotted at my mouth's left corner.

Yvonne Reddick

L'Art de vénerie

I'd pour him Saint Emilion dark as a clot,
as he chewed the breasts of wild pigeon
in their port-deepened juices,
savoured hart's flesh with redcurrants.

In this place where Master Forester
Bowbearer and Verderer
tended vert and venison,

we walked a Bowland ridge.
"Men are like stags," he said.
He coveted sixteen-branch hartshorns,
a doe-eyed harem milling at his hooves.

That smile creased his cheek
like old vellum: *The Art of Venery*.
He'd feel for the heart, point to aim, pierce
then thrust a practised coup de grace –
a bright tear in me blooded his sheets.

I bolted through the spinneys,
didn't pause until I reached the river.

Trash

My cup with its red-stained Styrofoam lip
that I wept into when I said I was moving
north, and would you come too?

My watch-clasp, which you undid one-handed
as our room echoed 'Tiger Mountain Peasant Song' –
the plastic pot of the orange bromeliad
you gave to me for an earlier birthday,

that outlasts leaves and anniversaries.
A millennium for my claret glass
and five centuries for the aluminium can
which blurted out your beer at that gig

where I first noticed your shoulders' breadth
in the houndstooth coat whose nylon will survive us, unbroken.

Yvonne Reddick

Sorrows of the Deer

My father lies face down
in the torrent that gouged Glen Spean.
Peat water brims
in the honeycombs of his lungs –
he has no gills to breathe.

I trace his last journey
from summit to valley,
stepping deerlike
from Corriechoille Farm

up the mottled hide
of the Peak of the Brawling Corrie,
down the heathery flanks
of the Hill of the Calf's Coombe

to peer into the stony cleuch
where the current churns.

Soon, I'm gaunt
as the wide-eyed cranium of a doe
or a new-dropped fawn
shivering in damp membranes.

The day after he died
a wild hind watched me
from the birches by the Spey,
pricked her dished ears towards me.

Gralloched and flayed,
my childhood hangs
in the vaulted game-larder
of a hoary laird.

I need to weather brunt winds,
stolid as a tor
where mizzle pools and trickles –
I am hornless,
the wind stings through my fur.

I need to root in granite,
grow to Suilven saxifrage
(Dad loved its rockbreaking name),
or a solid cairn
under a bluffart of snow.

Deerhart

That granite notch
in the Peak of the Pelts
is Ossian's – Fawn's – Cave.
I crouch under its dripping walls.

I want to endure,
a cup-and-ring marked stone
in Achnabreck –
the ancient landmap
of a spring's upwelling.

But a week into his death
I drive with my sister through Warfield
where a young roe
stares fly-eyed from the verge,
her neck wrenched.

The gully is lush
with bracken fronds,
pink pyramidal orchids –
a Bristows helicopter
spots Dad in an eddying pool,

a smirr of rain
stains the afternoon
as we commit him to fire, to air.

Under the rood screen
carved with scrolled ferns
we sing 'The Deer's Cry'.

Yvonne Reddick

My Grandmother Was A Pink-Footed Goose

I squint north –
clouds like the sails
of a goosewinging boat.

I blow on my fists,
feel the scrunched membrane
meshing index to thumb.
Nails press like quills,
as if each finger
could sprout a pinion
and my thumb could end
in a bastard wing.

Where are the flocks?

My Mémé was bird-bone hollow, all ribstrakes and flapping bald elbows, flesh slouched over a V of sternum. Shallow breath-râles, knuckly birdleg fingers. Her English evaporated as her mind nested the tumour. The remains: "J'ai ces ... hallucinations" of pools and oceans, my father webbing through air, his hands in outspread sheaves of primaries.

Plume-cinder ash when we burned Mémé. The south-easterly hush-hushed it north.

A horizon speck
sharpens into focus
as a wishbone V.
Flying at altitude,
geese pant each second,
their heartbeats must blur –
how do they snatch breath to call?

The names of their nest-sites
freeze air as I voice them:
Spitsbergen. Hvannalindir.

Touchdown of lipgloss feet
on saurian legs.
Parched beaks dapping
in algal-green pools.
The mere pours
off watermarked necks.

I wondered if anything could return
from those altitudes –

here are pink-footed geese
crying *hark hark.*